HARK! A VAGRANT

Library and Archives Canada Cataloguing in Publication: Beaton, Kate, 1983–. *Hark! A Vagrant* / Kate Beaton. ISBN 978-1-77046-060-7. I. Title. PN6733.B42H37 2011   741.5'971   C2011-901768-7.

Drawn & Quarterly acknowledges the financial contribution of the Government of Canada through the Canada Book Fund and the Canada Council for the Arts for our publishing activities and for support of this edition.

Published in the USA by Drawn & Quarterly, a client publisher of Farrar, Straus and Giroux. Orders: 888.330.8477. Published in the Canada by Drawn & Quarterly, a client publisher of Raincoast Books. Orders: 800.663.5714

HARK! A VAGRANT

KATE BEATON

DRAWN AND QUARTERLY · MONTRÉAL

Let me take a minute to dedicate this book to my parents, because it's the right thing to do with your first book, and no one deserves it better. Some time ago I packed my history degree into a suitcase and said goodbye to the world of working in museums for low pay and limited opportunity, and said hello to the world of being a cartoonist, which, as we all know, is lucrative and glamorous. I had been drawing comics since university, when I would put off essays for history classes to draw comics for the student paper. Not that I didn't enjoy my classes, rather the opposite, but you and I both know that there are always better things to be doing than writing an essay that's due by the end of the week. It turned out, to my great luck, that what I really had a knack for was putting the two together— history and comics. That's what started all this, in any case. I think comics about topics like history or literature can be amazing educational tools, even at their silliest. So if you learn or look up a thing or two after reading these comics, and you've enjoyed them, then I will be more than pleased! If you're just in it for the silly stuff, then there is plenty of that to go around, too. While I have the chance, I want to thank a few people. First, the authors whose work I read—whether it was a novel to be parodied, historical research, a comic book, or any number of things. I am forever in debt to those who have inspired, educated, and entertained me, and given life to my comics. Secondly, thanks to everyone who has supported me in this from the beginning—you friends, you family, you readers. You know, the thing that keeps you doing a job like this is the idea that there is someone out there who is actually going to like what you're making, and I can't believe I'm fortunate enough to have fantastic people who enjoy the loony pictures I like to draw. I'll keep it up for as long as I can, or until the museum world calls and begs to have me back...and they have a dental plan.

GET ME OFF THIS FREAKING MOOR

Anne, why are you writing books about how alcoholic losers ruin people's lives? Don't you see that romanticizing douchey behavior is the proper literary convention in this family! *Honestly*. Losers who ruin people's lives are who we want to dream about at night.

A HISTORY DEBATE

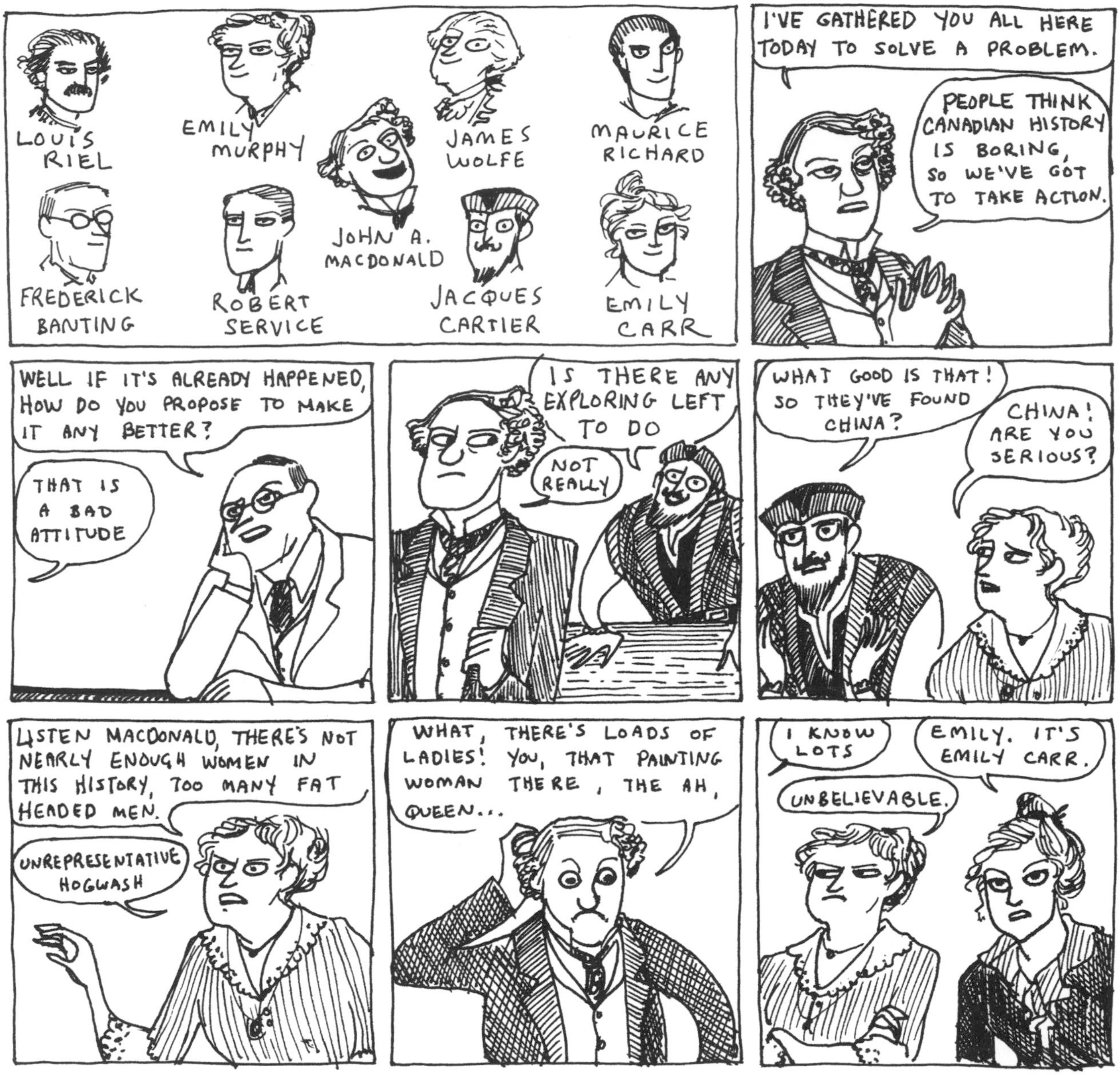
LOUIS RIEL
EMILY MURPHY
JAMES WOLFE
MAURICE RICHARD
FREDERICK BANTING
ROBERT SERVICE
JOHN A. MACDONALD
JACQUES CARTIER
EMILY CARR
I'VE GATHERED YOU ALL HERE TODAY TO SOLVE A PROBLEM.
PEOPLE THINK CANADIAN HISTORY IS BORING, SO WE'VE GOT TO TAKE ACTION.
WELL IF IT'S ALREADY HAPPENED, HOW DO YOU PROPOSE TO MAKE IT ANY BETTER?
THAT IS A BAD ATTITUDE
IS THERE ANY EXPLORING LEFT TO DO
NOT REALLY
WHAT GOOD IS THAT! SO THEY'VE FOUND CHINA?
CHINA! ARE YOU SERIOUS?
LISTEN MACDONALD, THERE'S NOT NEARLY ENOUGH WOMEN IN THIS HISTORY, TOO MANY FAT HEADED MEN.
UNREPRESENTATIVE HOGWASH
WHAT, THERE'S LOADS OF LADIES! YOU, THAT PAINTING WOMAN THERE, THE AH, QUEEN...
I KNOW LOTS
EMILY. IT'S EMILY CARR.
UNBELIEVABLE.

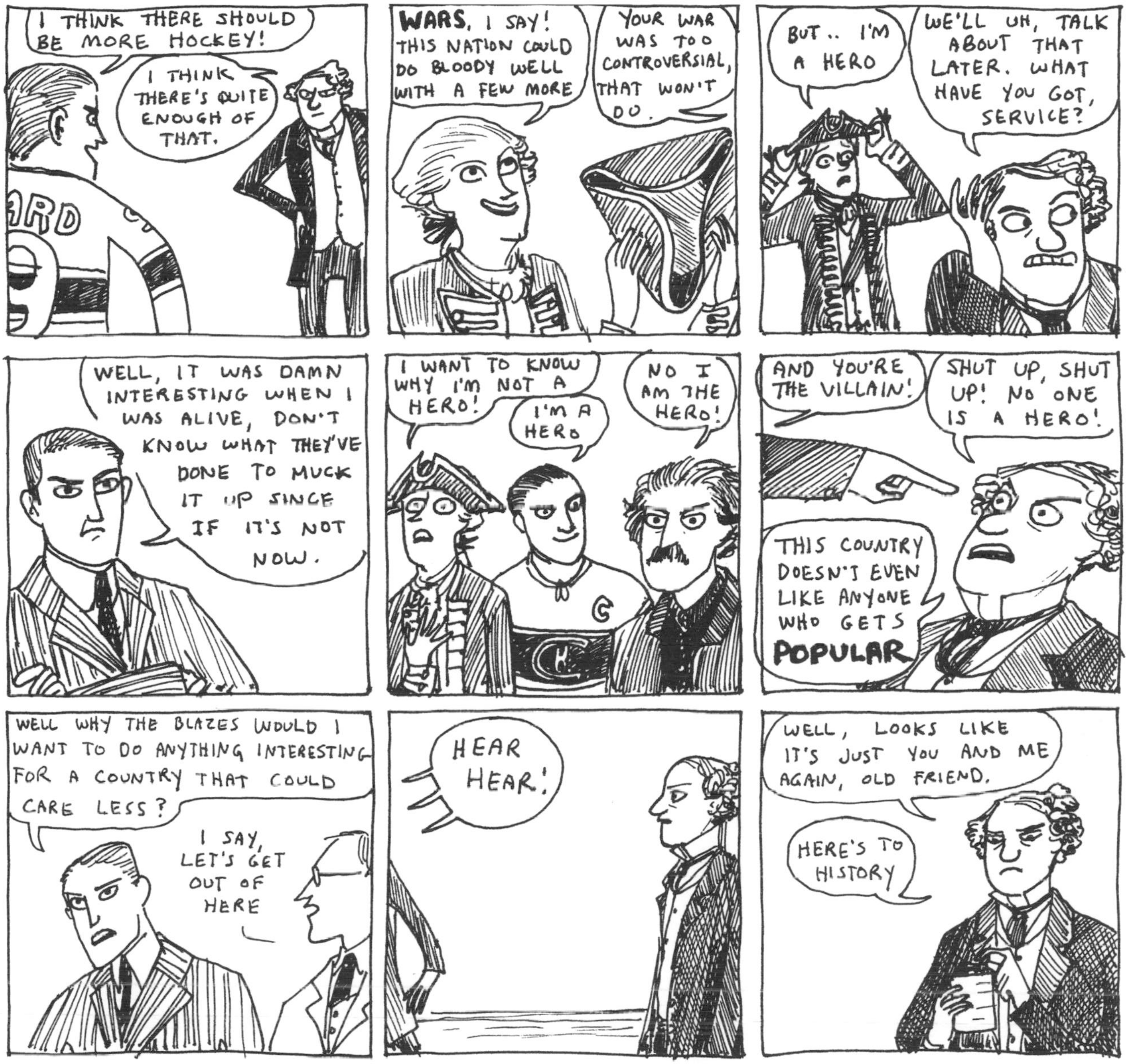
I THINK THERE SHOULD BE MORE HOCKEY!
I THINK THERE'S QUITE ENOUGH OF THAT.
WARS, I SAY! THIS NATION COULD DO BLOODY WELL WITH A FEW MORE
YOUR WAR WAS TOO CONTROVERSIAL, THAT WON'T DO.
BUT.. I'M A HERO
WE'LL UH, TALK ABOUT THAT LATER. WHAT HAVE YOU GOT, SERVICE?
WELL, IT WAS DAMN INTERESTING WHEN I WAS ALIVE, DON'T KNOW WHAT THEY'VE DONE TO MUCK IT UP SINCE IF IT'S NOT NOW.
I WANT TO KNOW WHY I'M NOT A HERO!
I'M A HERO
NO I AM THE HERO!
AND YOU'RE THE VILLAIN!
SHUT UP, SHUT UP! NO ONE IS A HERO!
THIS COUNTRY DOESN'T EVEN LIKE ANYONE WHO GETS POPULAR
WELL WHY THE BLAZES WOULD I WANT TO DO ANYTHING INTERESTING FOR A COUNTRY THAT COULD CARE LESS?
I SAY, LET'S GET OUT OF HERE
HEAR HEAR!
WELL, LOOKS LIKE IT'S JUST YOU AND ME AGAIN, OLD FRIEND.
HERE'S TO HISTORY

A MAGICAL DAY

My father is an excellent gardener and can grow enough vegetables to keep us fed all through the winter. Turnips are amazing because they are root vegetables, so if you pick them and put them in soil in the cellar, they last for ages and ages. For more information about turnips, see every day of my childhood.

If Susan B. Anthony were on *Sex and the City*, do you think she would be a Carrie, a Miranda, a Charlotte, or a Samantha? Definitely a Samantha.

JUST DON'T FLY DURING RED APRIL

In WWI, pilots were the cool new thing. So exciting! Flying aces! Nothing like that had ever existed before. That's why people like Billy Bishop could become a star and inspire all the young bros to sign up. The only real drawback was that for 99 percent of new recruits, an engine would blow up in their faces two minutes after taking off for the first time. Beyond that, it's a great life. Just don't fly during Red April, boys.

TEAM BOLIVAR

Sucre was Bolívar's right hand man for sure (matching hairdos and everything), but I think he had a much different approach to leadership. I really wonder how different the outcome of the Spanish American Wars of Independence would have been if Sucre hadn't been assassinated just as he was poised to become Bolívar's obvious successor. I wish I had something funny to say now.

PEARY I THOUGHT WE WERE FRIENDS

Peary got himself some frostbitten feet and someone else drove that sled and *that* is *that*. Now, these two weren't Canadian, but it is always interesting to note that at the very same time that Canadian immigration was insisting that black people couldn't handle the cold, a black man was the first non-native person to set foot on the North Pole. Don't you love it when the irony is that good? Matthew Henson gets his due these days; it only took a century or something. A nod to Ootah, Egingwah, Seegloo, and Ooqueah as well.

Poor Doctor Watson gets a bad hand in a lot of on-screen portrayals and parodies, and more than a few people have a mental image of him as a fat old dodderer. Unfair! We all look kind of stupid next to Sherlock Holmes, but come on.

ANOTHER CASE of WATSONS

Here's the thing about a homosexual relationship between Holmes and Watson: you are never going to prove it. It just isn't in the books, explicitly. It would be rad if it were, but it's not, so now we are going to have arguments with no end because, maybe maybe maybe maybe. Eventually the idea that these two were hookin' up between the pages gets so popular that people who never read the books will argue, "Yeah man, of course they were!" That's popular culture for you! It's interesting. Between you and me, I much prefer Gay Watson to Stupid Watson (I mean, obviously). What Watson does in his spare time is his business. Now solve me some damn crimes, boys!

I'll make one of those YA series where adults believe what teens tell them. Except instead of fake teens, mine will have real ones because real teens don't give a shit about anything.

Nothing says "Hallowe'en" like teens being punks and throwing shit. They're on the job here, but who knows what for. They're not doing it anyway, whatever it is.

Not their employer's office, another one! Oh you little teenage ne'er-do-wells. Like most teens, they go to school, but much like the ones who enroll in art class because it's easy, sometimes they are also not there.

BOWIE AND RONNO WANT AN ICE CREAM

THE PROSTITUTES ARE SO TIRED OF THIS SHIT

DO SOMETHING ABOUT IT

The Pony is an enduring symbol of...something in whatever country he lives in. It would be fascinating to know what that is or what the people see in him. Clearly though, I am not going to tell you.

PONY

The pony returns! It does a job for the king, I think. But that could all be in the king's head.

ANNE OF SLEEVES

In *Anne of Green Gables*, the plucky young orphan grows from a child with a wild imagination and a tongue she cannot hold into a sophisticated and responsible young lady. If there were no scene where she gets the puff-sleeved dress she pines for, I think there would have been a chapter where she slaughters the whole town.

Finally, after years of hard work, Handel broke through with his first major hit, "Safety Dance," and he totally ruled the eighties!!

THE SCOTTISH PLAY

They say the real Macbeth was a pretty decent fellow and a good ruler, and he'd probably have a bone to pick with Shakespeare over character assassination. He'd have to get in line behind Richard III though, whom I have heard (from certain Elizabethan sources) was an ugly hunchbacked troll.

UNSEX ME, SEX ME

THE GAG COMES BACK

HELL IS MURKY

MACBETH WANTS TO HEAR IT AGAIN

BANQUO'S SONS WILL BE KINGS, YES

EACH ONE WILL GET HANDSOMER AND HANDSOMER UNTIL KING JAMES I

DID THAT REALLY HAPPEN!!

YES

LAY ON MACDUFF, WITH MOTIFS

MACBETH, YOU ARE THROUGH!

ALLOW ME TO MAKE A COMMENT ON HOW YOU ARE WEARING CLOTHES THAT ARE TOO BIG FOR YOU.

AW COME ON THAT'S ALREADY BEEN DONE LIKE THREE TIMES

IT WILL BE A METAPHOR FOR HOW YOU ARE A BAD KING

GOOD QUESTION

I BRING THE HEAD OF MACBETH!

WHAT ARE YOU GOING TO DO WITH IT?

OH – I'M NOT SURE

THE RETURN of ANNABEL LEE

When I read *Annabel Lee* and listen to that narrator pine and whine and pine, I think "Man, Annabel? You put up with this loser?" It's okay to pine now and then, but the man needs a hobby that isn't lying beside her grave and moaning. Then I wonder, "What if Annabel came back and she was just as lame as he was?" It's like they say: be careful what you wish for.

COME DREAM WITH ME

It's true that Jules Verne wrote what we may call "fan mail" to Edgar Allan Poe. By fan mail, of course, I mean a full-on sequel to one of Poe's books. Perhaps Poe doesn't get enough credit for influencing science fiction, since many people think about ravens, madness, and other dreary things when the name "Poe" comes up. Don't get me wrong, the man could write a dirge of a paragraph, a hell of a wah-wah cryfest. But he could also write about hot air balloons.

Jules Verne made a famous rant about H.G. Wells once that basically threw a fit over Wells making up whatever he liked about spaceships and other devices. Wells wrote about these things without explicitly describing how they functioned, and he didn't power them with steam or coal or anything that made sense in 1899. Jules didn't like that! "It's science fiction," he said, "so where's the science?!" In response, Wells possibly called Verne "an old fusspot."

ONE OF YOU WILL DO IT BY GOD

Dynasties the monarchy way are so easy! You have a kid? Great, they are next in line for the best throne in the Throne Room. In America it's hard because you have to "prove yourself" and maybe people have to "vote for you" and that's difficult! No one knew that better than Joe Kennedy Sr., who trained his wife to give birth to the United States Senate.

PROTÉGÉ

Beethoven had an Immortal Beloved but no children to pass his wisdom onto. I guess he figured his nephew would have to do. Unfortunately for everyone in this comic, talent is not a thing you can pass on, nor passion for any one thing. Writing a fantastic symphony is not like baking Mom's secret pie recipe, even if Mom's secret pie recipe is pretty darn good.

CRIMINAL MASTERMINDS

I have no idea why I made them talk so funny, but that is what happens sometimes in this crazy comics world. I guess it is because it's a comic about two weirdos! Here we meet Burke and Hare toward the end of their killing spree, a period that may be described as "unbelievably sloppy" and also "lazy." Still, they had an impact on medical history (medical cadavers for everyone!), and perhaps not every harebrained criminal may lay claim to this.

Some fast comics. Out they come, pen to paper, lickety split.

CELEBRATE THE BEST WAY

Canadians are their most Canadian on three occasions: when they've left the country, when Olympic Hockey is going on, and on Canada Day. The rest of the time it's a toss-up on whether they're feeling patriotic or if they just feel like tossing the whole enterprise and moving to Miami. Anyway, what is a celebration of national unity in this country without a little national disunity? It's only proper, traditionally.

BE A HERO

Wonder Woman has spent a lifetime as one of the biggest deals in comics, and yet I think it's universally agreed that no one has been able to truly "get" her character right. If that were me, I'd probably be pissed.

WORLD'S FINEST

IT'S IN HIS NATURE

WONDER WOMAN RETURNS

Weren't most superheroes first created to fight Nazis? Guess they had to find something else to do after the war.

ONCE UPON A

Remember when you found out that fairy tales were much deeper and darker than the Disney cartoons you knew made them out to be? I mean, Cinderella's stepsisters are punished *how* in Grimm's version? You were like, "Damn!" when you read that. Perhaps you thought, "Maybe that's not such a bad thing, to jazz it up a bit?" Perhaps you even thought that the elves in *The Elves and the Shoemaker* were a major bore and would be better if they were members of the band Kiss.

BRUNEL IS TIRED OF THESE TIME TRAVELING ASSHOLES

FIRING SQUAD

SICK MANUSCRIPT BRO

ALSO IT IS MY PERSONAL FETISH

WW II HIPSTER BATALLION

WW II HIPSTER BATTALION

HIPSTERS RUIN EVERYTHING, PT. 1

It's funny when people complain about how hipsters ruined this or that as though if hipsters would just go away, the problem would be solved and you could go back to wearing plaid shirts like you did before they were ruined for everyone. Directionless youths have always appropriated things and made them annoying! You have it easy, oh reader! The Beats had walking caricatures to deal with, and Goethe had suicidal poet dandies on his doorstep.

HIPSTERS RUIN EVERYTHING, PT. 2

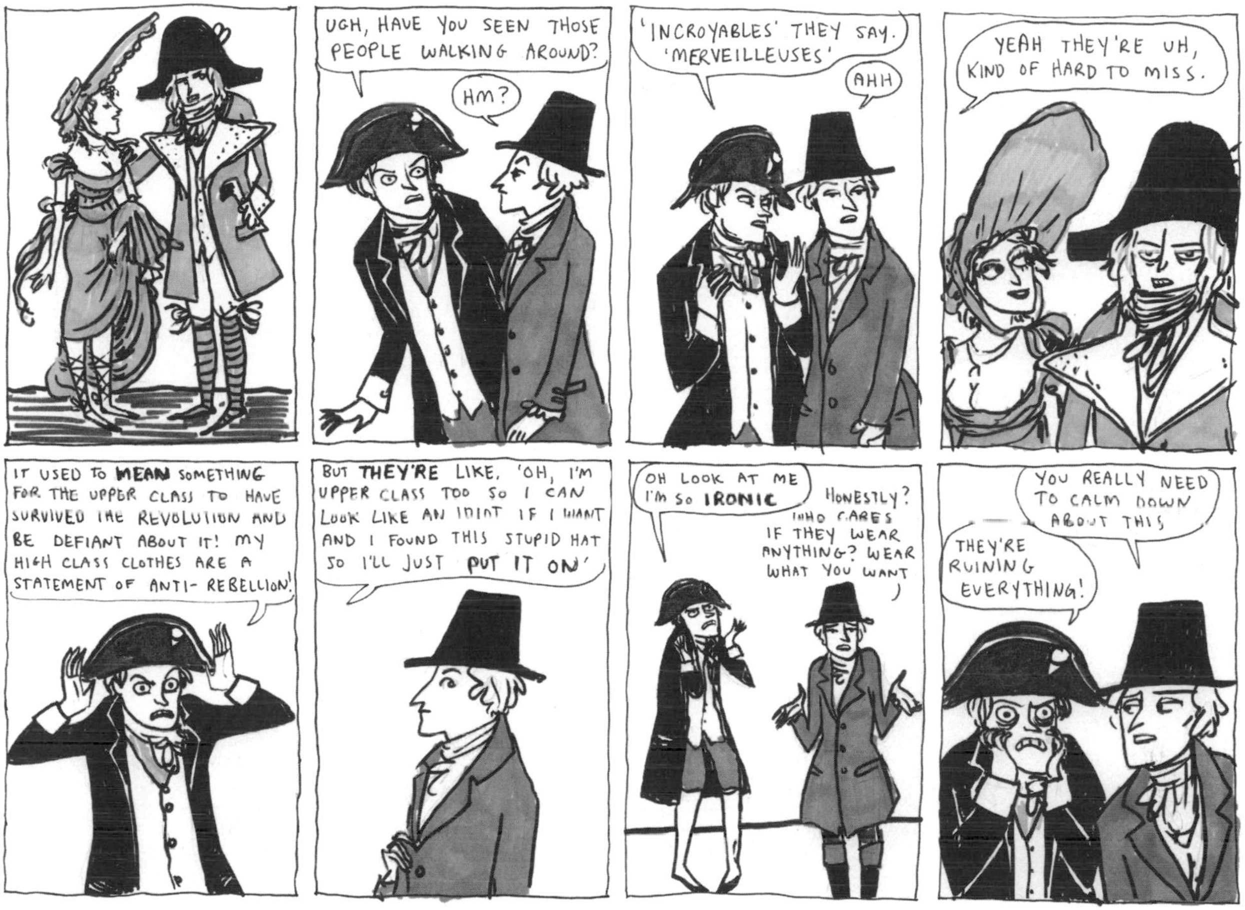
UGH, HAVE YOU SEEN THOSE PEOPLE WALKING AROUND?
HM?
'INCROYABLES' THEY SAY. 'MERVEILLEUSES'
AHH
YEAH THEY'RE UH, KIND OF HARD TO MISS.
IT USED TO MEAN SOMETHING FOR THE UPPER CLASS TO HAVE SURVIVED THE REVOLUTION AND BE DEFIANT ABOUT IT! MY HIGH CLASS CLOTHES ARE A STATEMENT OF ANTI-REBELLION!
BUT THEY'RE LIKE, 'OH, I'M UPPER CLASS TOO SO I CAN LOOK LIKE AN IDIOT IF I WANT AND I FOUND THIS STUPID HAT SO I'LL JUST PUT IT ON'
OH LOOK AT ME I'M SO IRONIC
HONESTLY? WHO CARES IF THEY WEAR ANYTHING? WEAR WHAT YOU WANT
THEY'RE RUINING EVERYTHING!
YOU REALLY NEED TO CALM DOWN ABOUT THIS

The Incroyables and Merveilleuses were ironic hipsters years before their time. What they wore was once a political statement, but then they gave up on making statements, and that was a statement.

TUDORAMA

It's weird when television and movies think that in order to reach a modern audience, they need to sex up history. Sexy people did live in the past, and they had sex! Maybe that's not enough. Someone needs to build a time machine and go tell William Cecil that he may have been a crack statesman, but if he wants us to give a shit about him, he better start hitting the gym.

THE DEATH OF GENERAL BROCK

At Queenston Heights there is a stunning monument to a man who would not order his men anywhere he would not lead them. Somehow, mysteriously, this man got himself shot by a sniper. By mysteriously, of course, I mean that everyone was largely dressed the same, except for the fellow in front with the giant hat, big brass buttons, and, oh I don't know, rippling epaulettes. And anyway, of course you're going to shoot that guy.

STRANGER

I CAME FOR THE DICK JOKES

46

IT'S HOW WE DID IT BACK THEN

SUBSTITUTE TEACHER

WRONG ISLAND

BIG BUSINESS

BEST FRIENDS FOREVER

MESSIN' WITH YOUR KIDS

NEWS FROM THE FRONT

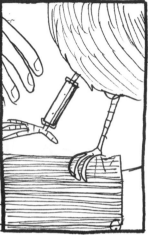

A BAD AFFAIR

REGRETS

I MARRIED A MANCHILD: 2063

DO YOU REMEMBER THE LOOK ON OUR SON'S FACE THE DAY HE GOT MARRIED

NOT REALLY

DO YOU REMEMBER THUNDERCATS

THAT WAS SUCH A GOOD SHOW

STUPID ROOSTER COMICS

LADAYS

AWE YEAH GIRL

YOU WANT DIS

THE OLD FOX

Is Montcalm less memorable because he lost the Battle of the Plains of Abraham to Wolfe? Unfair—I like Montcalm. All you need to know to like him as well is that his last letter to his wife reads, "I think I should have given up all my honors to be back with you, but the king must be obeyed; the moment when I shall see you again will be the finest of my life. Good-bye my heart, I believe I love you more than ever." What I am saying is that I want a romance novel with Montcalm on the cover and I want it now. He got one of those epic-death paintings eventually. It's okay.

EVERY LADY SCIENTIST WHO EVER DID ANYTHING TILL NOW

Rosalind! Don't let 'em get you down. The trouble with reading about any given woman who was born before your mom is that yes, sometimes, they were hilarious, powerful, tough, loud, etcetera, etcetera—all good comic making material! But then sometimes, man, the main thing about them is that they just got screwed, big time. Here's to all the old time ladies of science, and their ideas that were worth stealing.

AN EDUCATION

INTERVENTION

THE LATEST FASHIONS

CHARLES' POETRY

RADIUM EYES

THE TRUE FAITH

SCOUNDRELLY

Lord Lovat (Simon Fraser, born 1667—there are about a million Simon Fraser Lord Lovats) really epitomizes how reading Scottish history can make you want to tear your eyeballs out, or laugh because it's so nutty that it could pass as a farce. Either the people involved are disastrously loyal, or disastrously duplicitous. Everything is a disaster, but it's a hell of a ride. Lord Lovat was the last man to lose his head in Great Britain. I suppose, depending on whom you talk to, he deserved the honour.

Canadian stereotypes are either hilarious and amazing or stupid and embarrassing, depending on whom you ask. But I can't help myself. I love our silly stereotypes. Anyone who gets upset because too many people think their country is exceedingly polite needs to rethink their priorities. I want to apologize to anyone who is offended by that statement.

THE CANADIANS HEARD US MAKING FUN OF THEM, AND GOT ALL FUCKED UP ON HOCKEY
NOW THEY'RE HEADED THIS WAY! WE SHOULDN'T HAVE CALLED THEM BORING
WELL THEY ARE!
DON'T WORRY. I KNOW THEIR WEAKNESSES. THEY CAN'T HELP THEMSELVES.
WHY HELLO! IT'S SO NICE TO SEE YOU ALL!
IT'S... SO NICE TO BE HERE
...THANK YOU

BIRTHDAY

SOH-RY

FINALLY THE RIGHT LEADER

ST. FRANCIS AND THE BIRDS

Catholic children are usually brought up with picture books of Saints; sometimes they have a favorite one. Many have super scary stories, like, "Saint So-and-So was ripped to pieces and consumed by hot flames." You know, stuff kids can relate to. Consequently, a lot of children like St. Francis of Assisi the best because his deal is that he is always pictured surrounded by a load of animals and no one chopped his head off.

THE BRAVE CREW OF THE NAUTILUS BATTLE THE MONSTROUS SQUID

The Nautilus was actually attacked by a "poulpe," which is an octopus, but the description sounds something like a squid, and it's usually translated as "squid." Does that make a difference? If a creature from the depths were attacking your ship, would you really care if it was an octopus or a squid, or would you just pull the hatch down over your head and try to remember how to pray? There are no atheists in foxholes, or in submarines beset by many-legged monsters.

NED! THE HARPOON!
HA HA, WEE!
DONK
WELL DONE
WA-
NONE OF US WILL EVER FORGET THAT TERRIBLE SCENE...

PERIL

Thus did the Vikings terrorize the coast of Britain, among other places, joyously taking for themselves shiny trinkets and the newest styles in leggings, delighting in the suffering of others as they filled their pockets with scrunchies and fashion magazines.

LIKE I AM BUSY SETTING THINGS ON FIRE
OMIGOD NO YOU HAVE TO SEE THIS
ILLUMINATED MANUSCRIPT
OMIGAWD TO DIE FOR
DID YOU EVEN SEE THE COMMUNION CHALICE I FOUND?
OMIGOD OMIGOD OMIGOD
DEAR DIARY - LINDISFARNE TRIP
SO AMAZING

MATRICIDE

There are some funny things in *The Life Of Nero*, if you like your maniac emperors that way. Pretty well all accounts of how Nero went about murdering his mother are hilariously awful in their own right—collapsible boat, anyone?—and the notion that he thought her ghost was after him is also good. On top of this, he had a neck beard, and according to Suetonius, he had a mullet and smelled bad.

15th CENTURY PEASANT ROMANCE COMICS

WELL NEITHER HAS SHE

TAKE ME AWAY

Back in the day, things were harder, you know? Love was harder. One day your sweetheart is here, the next they get one of those diseases we only read about in *Ripley's Believe It Or Not!*

FOR THE GLORY OF LOVE

OR MAYBE LIVE TILL YOU'RE 40

OR BEAR BAITING

SEVERAL INCONGRUITIES IN THIS ONE

CREDIT WHERE CREDIT IS DUE

These days Tesla is enjoying a belated surge in popularity. Everyone seems to be on Tesla's side now, against Edison; whereas before, Edison was the hero and Tesla was some nut job making a different lightbulb. Edison is getting to be well known as the jerk he totally was! But let us never forget: he wasn't the only one, as Marconi demonstrates for us. I bet there is a ton of shit Tesla invented that got stolen by other people. Probably cool things like skateboards and helicopters. Patent your inventions, kids.

GOREYS

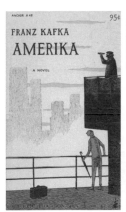

Edward Gorey made many a nice book in his day, and on top of this, designed many a nice book cover. We're going to do a little exercise with some of them. You take a book, and then you guess what the story inside of it is based on the info you get from the cover. Because, you know, that's just how books work.

Anchor A 15
95¢
LOVING
A novel by HENRY GREEN
A Doubleday Anchor Book
ARE THEY... LESBIANS?
DO THEY DO IT?
ARE THEY GONNA DO IT RIGHT NOW

ANTON CHEKHOV
ST. PETER'S DAY
AND OTHER TALES
HAPPY ST. PETER'S DAY MY FRIENDS!
POW POW POW POW POW POW POW POW
I NEVER KNOW WHAT THE FUCK IS HAPPENING ON ST PETER'S DAY BUT I LOVE IT
YOU'RE THE WINNER!

THE AUTOBIOGRAPHY OF WILLIAM BUTLER YEATS
WHEN WILLIAM BUTLER YEATS WAS BORN HE WAS A GIANT BIRD!!
CRAAA
EVERYONE WAS LIKE **WHOAA** BUT THEN HE WROTE SOME POEMS
CRAAAH
THESE ARE PRETTY GOOD

ANCHOR A14
95¢
THE WANDERER
A NOVEL BY
ALAIN-FOURNIER
THERE I CAME UPON AN ENCHANTED WOOD
AND THE MAGICAL SLUTS OF THE FOREST
HELLO
HI
OH WHAT AN ADVENTU WE
GRANDPA'S STORIES ARE **NOT TO BE LISTENED TO**

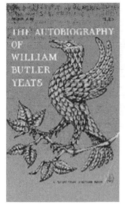

TRUE TALES FROM THE ANNALS OF CRIME AND RASCALITY BY ST. CLAIR MCKELWAY
COME LET ME TELL YOU A TALE OF CRIME AND RASCALITY
COME ... CLOSER
MY WALLET!
Anchor A-210
Selections from the Writings of
KIERKE-GAARD
Translated by Lee M. Hollander
A Doubleday Anchor Book
KIERKE GAARD

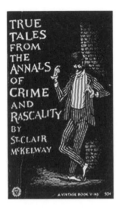

Signet Classic
The Woman In White
WILKIE COLLINS
One of the greatest thrillers of all time
now a MYSTERY! television presentation

THIS IS THE ADDRESS FOR THE WEDDING! OH WHERE IS THE CHURCH
OVER HERE!
THAT IS A VERY SMALL CHURCH

ANCHOR A31
75¢
HAMLET AND ŒDIPUS
A classic study in the psychoanalysis of literature
ERNEST JONES
A DOUBLEDAY ANCHOR BOOK

HAMLET! WHAT ARE YOU DOING, HERE?
OEDIPUS?
MUST BE SOME BOOK ABOUT WANTING TO BANG YOUR MOTHER
GOD! CAN'T THEY TALK ABOUT ANYTHING ELSE?

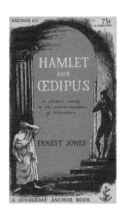

ANCHOR A38
GREEK TRAGEDY
A LITERARY STUDY BY
H.D.F. KITTO

MY HOME! IT IS DESTROYED!
WHAT WILL I DO?
OH WOW, A TRAGEDY
YOUR OUTFIT I MEAN.
FASHION POLICE!

An ELIZABETHAN SONG BOOK
LUTE SONGS: Madrigals & Rounds
Music edited by NOAH GREENBERG
Text edited by W. H. AUDEN and CHESTER KALLMAN

SHOT THROUGH THE HEART!
AND THOU'ST TO BLAME

WELL YOU'VE WON. YOU CAN HAVE SPAIN, OR PARTY ISLAND

PARTY ISLAND!

WHAT— THERE'S NOTHING HERE! PARTY ISLAND **SUCKS**

YEAH THEY NAMED IT PARTY ISLAND AS A JOKE.

IRONIC LIKE

WHAT HAVE I DONE

IT WAS FUNNY BUT I GUESS YOU HAD TO BE THERE

PATTY CAKE PATTY CAKE B— TROILUS...

WE'RE TOO **OLD** FOR THIS GAME

LET'S HAVE **SEX**

NO!. AGAIN!

BUT—

PATTY CAKE PATTY CAKE BAKER'S MAN!

THE AMBASSADORS
Henry James
A DOUBLEDAY ANCHOR BOOK
WE ARE HERE TO NEGOTIATE PEACE
I AM THE AMBASSADOR OF HUGS
AUGH, THIS IS... AWKWARD — WHAT ARE YOU THE AMBASSADOR OF?
YOU'LL SEE

A133
$1.45
A HERO OF OUR TIME
A NOVEL BY
MIHAIL LERMONTOV
Translated by Vladimir Nabokov in collaboration with Dmitri Nabokov
A DOUBLEDAY ANCHOR ORIGINAL
EXCUSE ME, ARE YOU A HERO? 'CAUSE I'VE BEEN LOOKING AND —
NO, NO, NOT ME
WELL WHAT ARE YOU DOING AT THIS VISTA PEERING OUT AS THOUGH INTO DESTINY?
OH UH, JUST HANGING OUT. I GUESS.
WELL WAY TO BE FREAKING SYMBOLIC!
I'm sorry!

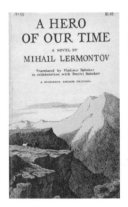

JOHN BELLAIRS
The Secret of the Underground Room
THIS UNDERGROUND ROOM IS GOING TO BE AMAZING
MOM? DAD?
BOYS
THIS IS WHERE YOU WERE CONCEIVED
DAD!

Anchor A8
95¢
The Secret Agent
A Novel by
Joseph Conrad
A Doubleday Anchor Book
CONGRATS, YOU GOT THE LIFETIME ACHIEVEMENT AWARD FOR BEING THE BEST SECRET AGENT
THANKS
MAN, I CAN'T BELIEVE HE STILL THINKS HE'S A SPY
30 YEARS IS TOO LONG FOR THIS JOKE, GUYS
HA HA HA
GIVE - GIVE HIM ANOTHER RAISE
MAYBE YOU SHOULD STOP
pfff hahaha

MASTERPIECES OF MYSTERY AND SUSPENSE
COMPILED BY MARTIN H. GREENBERG

THE FINDINGS ARE CONCLUSIVE. AFTER ALL THIS TIME...
SIR HUGH IS THE FATHER, NOT LORD FREDERICK
YES
BOO
HA HA YES YES YES
SOB

THE MASTERS
A NOVEL BY C. P. SNOW
A DOUBLEDAY ANCHOR BOOK

THEY SAY YOU'RE GOOD, BUT ARE YOU GOOD ENOUGH TO JOIN US?
JUST TELL HIM TO DROP A BEAT, WILL YOU!
THAT'S PRETTY SICK, YOU HAVE TO ADMIT
B-TS-B-TS
BM BM
KCH TS KCHH

C50 A DOUBLEDAY DOLPHIN MASTER
TALES OF THE GROTESQUE AND ARABESQUE
EDGAR ALLAN POE
FICTION
I KNOW WHAT YOU'RE THINKING
IS 'ARABESQUE' A RACIST THING, LIKE 'ORIENTAL'?
STAY TUNED
A DOUBLEDAY IMAGE BOOK 85¢
FELIX TIMMERMANS
THE PERFECT JOY OF ST. FRANCIS
A BIOGRAPHICAL NOVEL
"A perfect joy of a book." — BOOKS ON TRIAL
COMPLETE AND UNABRIDGED
IMAGE D11
THANK YOU MY FRIENDS, YOU BRING ME EVERYTHING I NEED
PAPERS TOO? YOU'RE THE BEST
ZIG ZAG

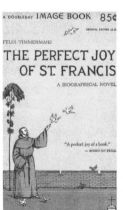

LAURA

Laura Secord looms so largely as a Canadian Hero (or as a box of chocolates depending on what your interests are), but during her lifetime, she fought until she was an old lady for anyone to recognize what she did at all. That sort of thing happened all the time; they can make a book about it called *Bummer History*. Good chocolates though.

THE ONE COMMANDMENT

MY PEOPLE I BRING YOU A MESSAGE FROM THE LORD!

GET DOWN GET DOWN GET DOWN TONITE

HE REALLY NEEDS TO FOCUS

HELP ME HANDSOME DOCTOR

HANDSOME DOCTOR, I'M SICK

DOES THIS HELP

NO

WHAT ABOUT THIS

NO

WELL THERE IS NOTHING I CAN DO FOR YOU

THE WISEST

I KNOW OWLS ARE WISE BUT WHICH ONE DO YOU THINK IS THE WISEST

OWLS

WELL, THAT ONE HAS A BEARD

OH HE MUST BE **VERY** WISE

OCEANS IN NEED

There's an idea out there that Aquaman is lame as far as superheroes go, but I'm not sure. I read a bit about Aquaman growing a beard and having a harpoon hand and living in a cave and talking to spirits or something, and thought, "How can anyone not like this guy? This crazy dude, living under the water?" Anyway, that is the only version of Aquaman that I know, but I am really into it.

PIRATES

YOU AND I COULD MAKE A BAD VENGEANCE

TATTOO COMPARISONS

Pirates are overdone these days. If you agree, please do not read the comics above.

I WANTED TO GET INTO FORENSICS BECAUSE OF CSI

NEMESIS MINE

AUSTEN MANIA

IT'S A LARGE BOOK

EMILY HAS SOME ADVICE

WHERE THIS IS GOING

Jane Austen has transcended "fandom," I think. Now there is an Austen culture. It's never certain what we should make of it. What is it about Mister Darcy that drove readers wild? What is it about the manners and conversation in the stories that inspired a craze of popular parodies? Why not a culture around, I don't know, *Madame Bovary*? Jane, either you are blessed, or you are cursed.

Are any of us really surprised that there is so much Darcy/Elizabeth fan fiction out there? Fan fiction was created for this. Aching stares from across the room can only go so far, if you know what I'm sayin'.

THE ROCHESTER WEDDING PARTY

In the various essays out there titled "In Defense of Mr. Rochester," we are to understand that keeping a nutty wife in your attic was a reasonable alternative to the asylums of the day. Fair enough. However, after much consideration, we the jury still find Mr. Rochester to be a creepy wife-hiding weirdo. We know Jane is coming back to him eventually, but we really wish Bertha could make a break for it.

JANE EYRE

GOOD TO BE UGLY

YOU EXAMINE ME, MISS EYRE, DO YOU THINK ME HANDSOME?

NO SIR

WELL GOOD! BECAUSE YOU'RE UGLY TOO

GOOD THEN WE ARE BOTH UGLY

THE SOLUTION

SO I LOCKED MY WIFE IN THE ATTIC AND SLEPT MY WAY THROUGH EUROPE SPENDING HER FORTUNE

IT WAS HARD. IT WAS I WHO SUFFERED

JANE DO YOU THINK I HAD A **CHOICE**

DO YOU?

THEN I FOUND THIS SELF HELP BOOK

BIGAMY ~THE~ ANSWER TO ALL YOUR PROBLEMS

What the heck is happening out on those moors? Is it like when you're out in your boat for too long and you start to lose it, and you think you see a beautiful mermaid, but it's really a manatee? Then you've made out with it and you don't know why? We only want Jane to be happy though, because she had a pretty rough go in life and she's a smart cookie. We'll let her have Mr. Rochester because she loves him, even though he might be a manatee.

WHAT WERE YOU THINKING

TRUEST DECLARATION

JEALOUSY

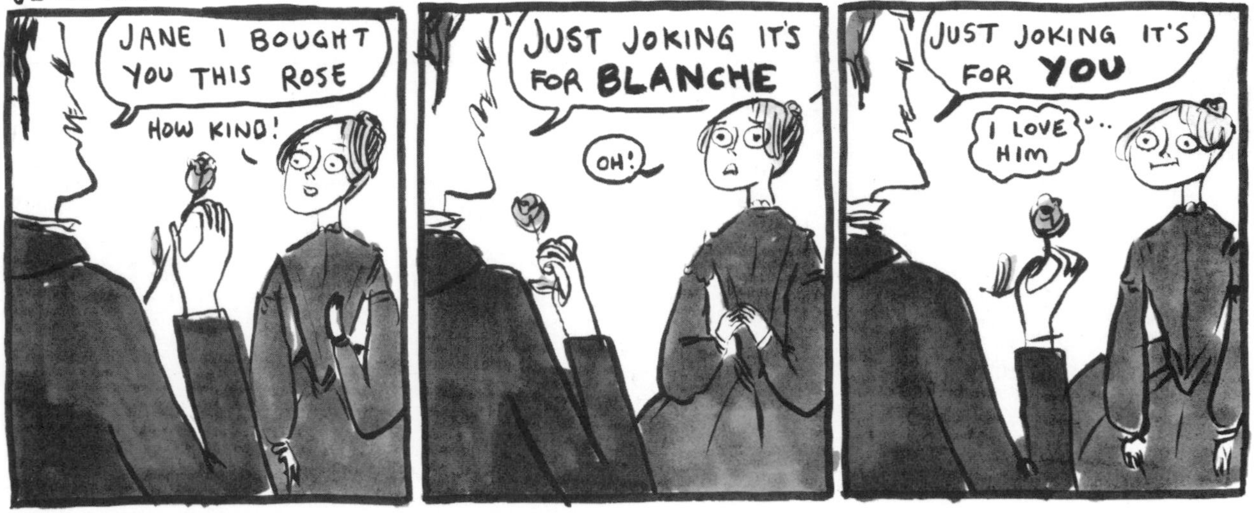
JANE I BOUGHT YOU THIS ROSE
HOW KIND!
JUST JOKING IT'S FOR BLANCHE
OH!
JUST JOKING IT'S FOR YOU
I LOVE HIM

HAPPY ENDING

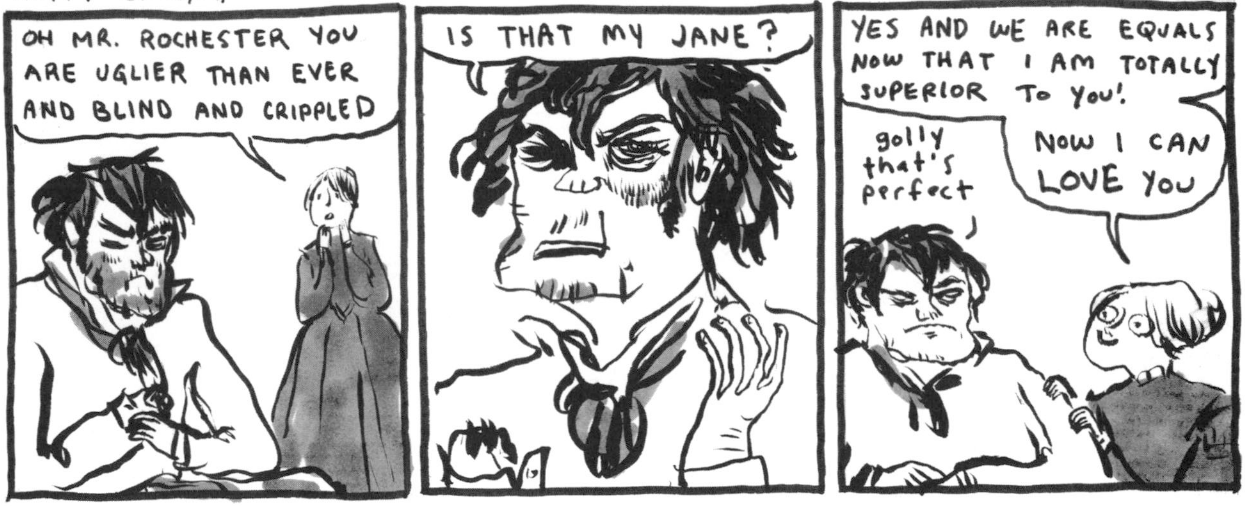
OH MR. ROCHESTER YOU ARE UGLIER THAN EVER AND BLIND AND CRIPPLED
IS THAT MY JANE?
YES AND WE ARE EQUALS NOW THAT I AM TOTALLY SUPERIOR TO YOU!
golly that's perfect
NOW I CAN LOVE YOU

DIRTY WORDS

TYCHO

VICTORIANS

Remember when you were small and you would lookup all the dirty words in the dictionary? If it were a good dictionary, it had at least three, and then you and your friends would laugh because dirty words are hi-larious. I resist the urge to put them in comics most of the time these days, but sometimes you just gotta (sorry Mom!).

WHAT A STUPID COMIC I HAVE MADE

FRANKLIN, AMERICA NEEDS YOU TO INVENT MORE AMAZING AND USEFUL THINGS

NO

I'M DEVOTING ALL MY TIME TO WHORES FROM NOW ON

WHAT COULD HAVE BEEN

NEMESIS RETURNS

SIR WE'RE TAKING MORE WATER THAN WE CAN HANDLE

THAT LAST CANNON VOLLEY WAS TOO MUCH

WE'RE GOING **DOWN** IT'S JUST **LIKE** HIM TOO, YOU KNOW?

MYTHICAL TEENS

ICARUS MY SON, THESE WINGS ARE A PRIVILEGE, NOT A RIGHT. DO NOT FLY TOO CLOSE TO THE SUN.

YO ICARUS

DO IT

HA HA MAN DO IT

HA HA YOU GUYS NOT IN FRONT OF MY DAD

PLEASE DO NOT LISTEN TO YOUR LOSER FRIENDS

PUG COMICS

WHO'S MOMMY'S BABY WITH A SQUISHY FACE! LITTLE CUTE SQUASHED IN FACE!

HOW DID YOU GET THIS NUMBER

How did he get that number?! A few liberties may have been taken in this comic. Bell and Watson probably did not have a direct line to Gray's newly developed telephone, but there it is nonetheless. Bell, ever the competitor, was in the airplane races as well as the telephone one and probably a bunch of others like the can-opener race and the whatever-hot-inventors-at-the-time-were-up-to race.

THE VERY CANADIAN REBELLION OF UPPER CANADA

WHAT WE **NEED** IS A REBELLION!

HEAR HEAR!

JUST A SMALL ONE. I DON'T WANT TO MAKE A FUSS

THEY'LL GET THE IDEA

HURRAH!

EDITORIAL CARTOON

HEY ST. PETER! I WAS A CELEBRITY. BUT I DIED.

A CELEBRITY!

I'M SUPPOSED TO SAY SOMETHING FUNNY

TAKE YOUR TIME

SHOW SOME RESPECT

WHERE IS THE JESTER, I COULD DO WITH SEEING SOME POINTLESS NONSENSE

HONEY, **PLEASE!** THE MAN IS AN **ARTIST**

A DURP DURP

ODYSSEUS AND HIS CREW ENCOUNTER THE FACEBOOK PERIL

JOCK CITY ELECTIONS

FRENCH REVOLUTION COMICS

A DAY RUINED

INAPPROPRIATE

Ah, the French Revolution. It's one of those things where the utter madness of it all lends itself to great comedy, usually of the madcap variety. I guess your large-scale terrors are easier to handle if someone is slipping on a banana peel.

SEND US YOUR REFERENCES

I JUST LIKE DRAWING BABIES

OPEN MIC NIGHT AT THE REVOLUTION

I'M SURE YOU UNDERSTAND

JOHN ADAMS LIGHTENS UP

John Adams was a grouchy old fellow who enjoyed being cantankerous the whole time that he was doing important things, which is a hard way to make friends. In *1776* the musical there is a whole song number where everyone is telling John Adams to sit down and shut up because they would rather be doing anything else in the world other than listen to him talk about even more things he's unhappy with. But Adams's stubborn ways have earned him a lot of fans who realize he was a cool dude in spite of it all. And really, isn't it time we just let the man relax a little?

JACKSON

CLEAN MY BOOTS

OLD HICKORY

Andrew Jackson: you love him or hate him, and not much in between. He did some good things. He brought himself up from nothing and did what he thought was best. And he did a lot of bad things. Modern folks can't really look at something like the Indian Removal Act and think, "Yeah, but maybe he was an okay dude." Don't kid yourselves either—it's not like in his time no one thought to duke it out with him when he was being a jerk. The man had so many musket balls in his body you could stick magnets to him, if magnets stuck to lead.

IT WAS A GIFT

YOU KNOW, JEFFERSON WAS OPPOSED TO THE IDEA OF POLITICAL PARTIES

WELL WHO CARES WHAT HE THOUGHT

HAHA OH AND ONCE HE HAD A GIANT BLOCK OF CHEESE AT THE WHITE HOUSE BE I'll SHOW **HIM**

HA HA

LYNCOYA

YOU'RE NOT MY REAL DAD! I DON'T HAVE TO LISTEN TO YOU!

YOU'RE JUST ANGRY BECAUSE I SLAUGHTERED YOUR BIRTH PARENTS BEFORE I ADOPTED YOU

WELL YOU'RE JUST GOING TO HAVE TO GET OVER THAT!

ATTEMPTED MURDER

MAN OF THE PEOPLE

EXTRA EXTRA

This isn't to say that all early political cartoons didn't belabor the point; rather, a good deal of them had several figures in view, with an entire paragraph each coming out of their mouths. Underneath the picture was, naturally, a lengthy explanation of the joke and/or main idea. A few of them managed to be pretty sick burns all the same.

GANGSTERS

SO DARLIN, DARLIN STAND

DAVY JONES, I MEAN, IN THE DRINK

We see something in gangsters that we like. They are all dangerous and cool and there are guns and money and cars and booze and all that stuff that is great for movies and bad for anything else. A tommy gun is such an iconic thing that you'd almost think it doesn't even shoot real bullets. The car just drives by, with someone hanging out, pointing the tommy gun at you and it just goes "rat-a-tat-tat-tat!" while you stand right where you are and cheer because you are crazy.

SLEEPTIME

NYEH! SEE?
HE'S HAVING A BAD DREAM
YOU RAT
OR A GOOD ONE
MAA

SURPRISE

HAPPY BIRTHDAY
I WAS EXPECTING A GIRL
TWENTY YEARS WE'VE KNOWN EACH-OTHER
AND NOW YOU DON'T WANNA SEE ME JUMP OUTTA DA CAKE
YOU INSULT ME

COURTLY LOVE

Courtly Love—so pure, so true! More pining than what the modern couple would care to indulge in, but pining is better than being bored to tears at your loom, I suppose. They say it was platonic, in that I-love-you-but-will-never-touch-you way, which seems about as likely as my platonic relationship with the Loch Ness Monster (we're just friends you guys).

GIFT WARS

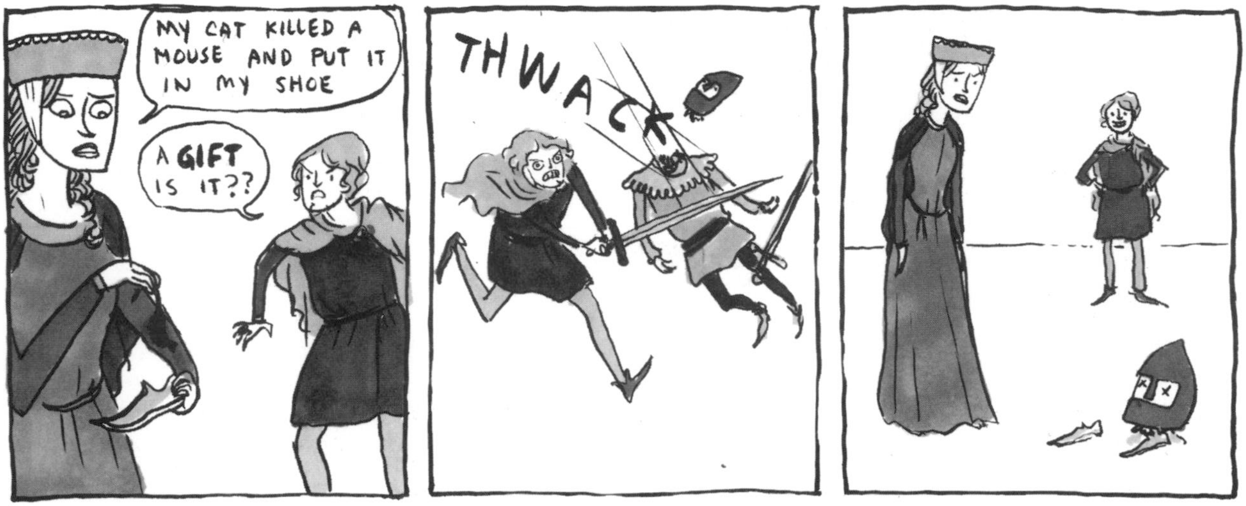
MY CAT KILLED A MOUSE AND PUT IT IN MY SHOE
A **GIFT** IS IT??
THWACK

INTUITION

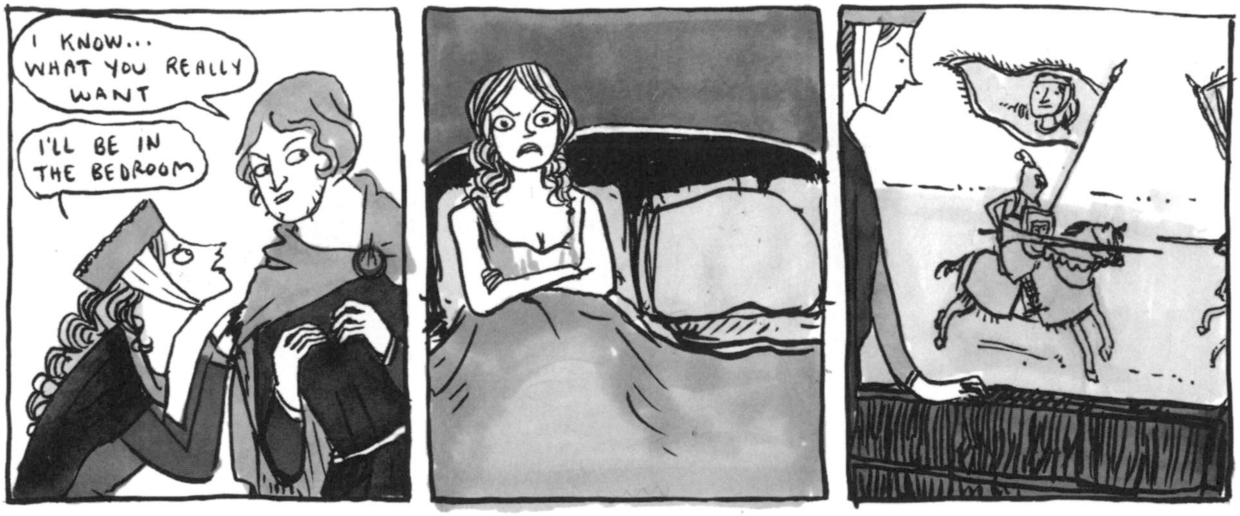
I KNOW... WHAT YOU REALLY WANT
I'LL BE IN THE BEDROOM

MY FAIR LADY

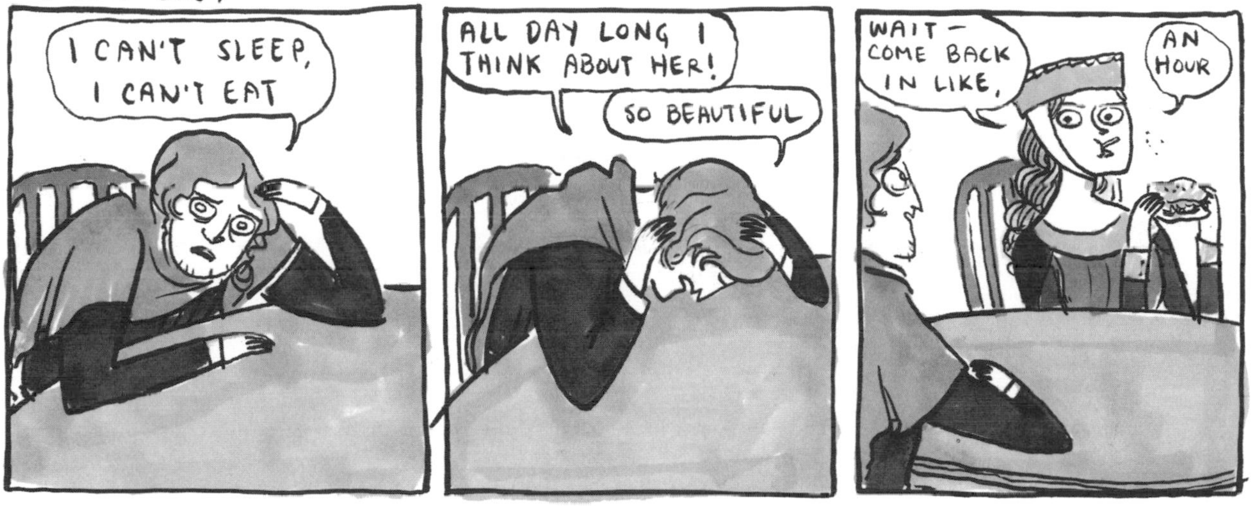
I CAN'T SLEEP, I CAN'T EAT
ALL DAY LONG I THINK ABOUT HER!
SO BEAUTIFUL
WAIT — COME BACK IN LIKE,
AN HOUR

SWEET SIGN OF AFFECTION

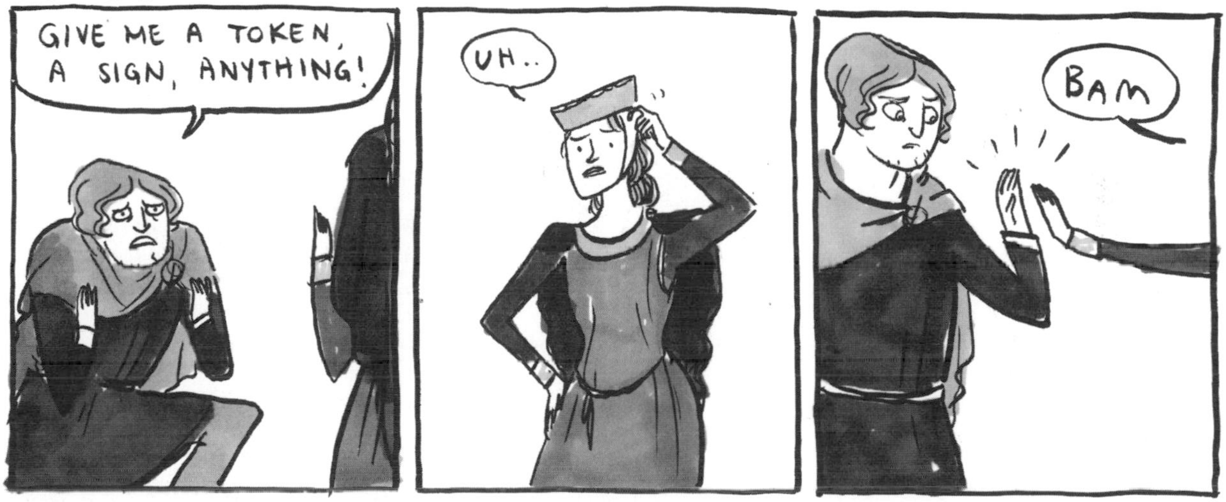
GIVE ME A TOKEN, A SIGN, ANYTHING!
UH..
BAM

BORGIAS

Lucrezia gets a bad rap for being a good-looking lady with a dubious family during a time when that set-up meant your life was going to be scandalous whether you liked it or not! They say she had a good deal of administrative sense when it came down to it, but let's face it, that's boring news compared to your father marrying you off to all his business contacts and your brother killing them.

THE MADNESS OF KING LEAR

UNREASONABLE

A WATCHED POT NEVER BOILS

King Lear is based on the life of an old king named Leir who occupies a nebulous sort of space as far as being sure of how much of his story is the real deal. We can be wary I guess, but if Old King Cole might have been a real person (*really?*), then Leir deserves a fighting chance as much as the next legendary figure.

JUST LIKE THE YMCA

CAMEO

REASON IN MADNESS

LEAR HAS GONE SO FAR INTO HIS MADNESS, HE BEGINS TO MAKE SENSE!

I WROTE A DICTIONARY

MAYBE NOT THAT MUCH SENSE

GOOD IDEA

CORDELIA YOU KNOW WE COULD PROBABLY JUST LIVE IN A BIRDCAGE TOGETHER FOREVER

OH, MAN, DAD THAT SOUNDS AWESOME

LET'S JUST UH..

GO FOR A LITTLE WALK FIRST

CRAZY ACRES

YOUNG ADA LOVELACE

Poor young Ada. The vices of poetry were all around, and within her very blood! If I were the Lady Isabella and had to deal with Lord Byron swinging dark moods around the house and swinging what was in his pants around every human or non-human item, I might have a bad opinion of The Arts as well. Isabella was a bit of a whiz with a protractor herself anyway, we are told. Later of course, Ada became famous for doing some computery things with Charles Babbage, the mechanics of their work on the Analytical Engine being something most of us still can't completely grasp, probably because our parents didn't mind if we read a poem now and then. Thus, no doubt, our mathematical ruin.

DRACULA

DON'T GO TO THE CASTLE

HAIRY PALMS ARE A GOOD SIGN AMIRITE

Here we have Bram Stoker's *Dracula*, a book written to tell ladies that if you're not a submissive waif, society goes to hell and ungodly monsters are going to turn you into child-killing horrors and someone is going to drive a bowie knife through your heart/cut off your head/etcetera. As you deserve! Thanks, Bram! I wrote it down so as to remember it. Also: foreigners. Not sure about those guys, *amirite*? Bram's got all the tips.

THE HORROR OF THE NEW WOMAN

WHAT A TRANSFORMATION

DRACULA COMES TO ENGLAND

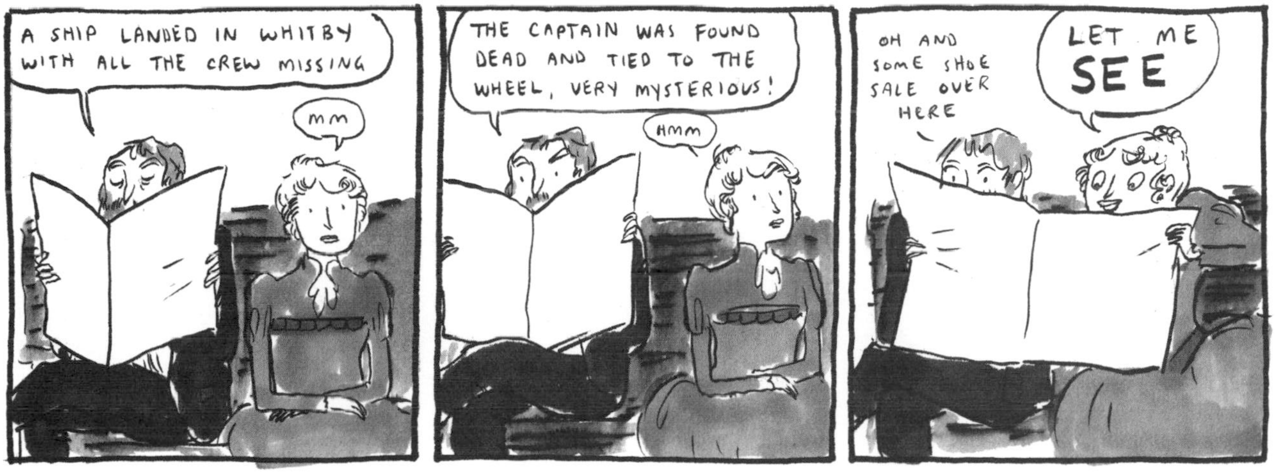
A SHIP LANDED IN WHITBY WITH ALL THE CREW MISSING
MM
THE CAPTAIN WAS FOUND DEAD AND TIED TO THE WHEEL, VERY MYSTERIOUS!
HMM
OH AND SOME SHOE SALE OVER HERE
LET ME SEE

FIFTY BOXES OF EARTH

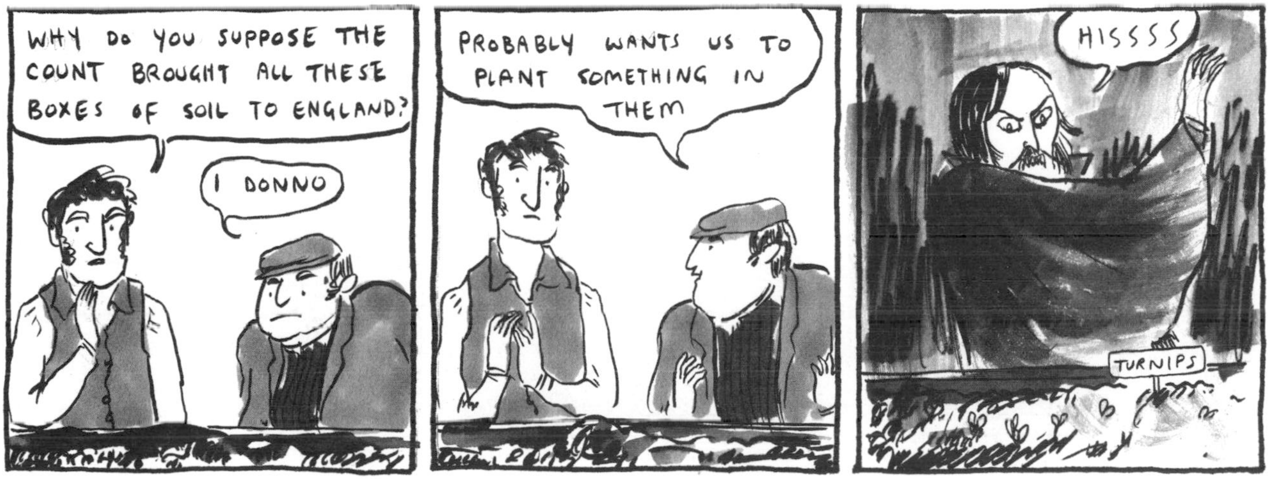
WHY DO YOU SUPPOSE THE COUNT BROUGHT ALL THESE BOXES OF SOIL TO ENGLAND?
I DONNO
PROBABLY WANTS US TO PLANT SOMETHING IN THEM
HISSSS
TURNIPS

HOT HOT METAPHORS

FOOLPROOF

CRUSOE

SHIPWRECK

TODAY, A STRANGE MAN WASHED UP ON THE BEACH

HE WAS ALIVE.

I THINK HE COMES FROM THE LAND OF NO BATHS

You smell like feet

EDUCATION

HE KEEPS TRYING TO TEACH ME HIS WORDS

uu AHem! Hemæourr ʏɑu Blahoɴɴɑu...

No thanks

AT THE SAME TIME, HE HAS NO IDEA HOW GOOD MY JOKES ARE. THAT'S TOO BAD.

Heh hah hah

Robinson Crusoe has been a children's favorite for years and years. I read it as a child and distinctly recall the impression that Crusoe and Friday were pretty good friends! Crusoe and Friday, chumming it up on the island, bonfires and Good Times. Obviously though, that notion was a little lopsided. There is that scene where Crusoe puts his foot on Friday's head and says he owns him and uh, well there's also the whole book.

NICE THREADS

TODAY THE STINKY MAN MADE SOME NEW CLOTHES FOR HIMSELF

Hmm

I GUESS

AFFECTION

RECENTLY HE'S TAKEN TO PATTING ME ON THE HEAD

WHAT IS HE, MY DAD?

DOOT DOOT and FRIDAY Bla am .. e HUR

I'M GOING TO KICK HIM IN THE NUTS

QUIT IT

MANIFEST DESTINY

BUT I THOUGHT WE WERE FRIENDS

JAVERT

JAVERT CHASES A GHOST

JAVERT CELEBRATES

Forget Jean Valjean—Javert is the real money in *Les Miserables*. Javert is like a robot in a cast of humans, not computing anything except data, not executing any motion except on the program he's running. When they finally make cyborg police, every one of them will operate like Javert and then you'll be sorry you ever even looked at that loaf of bread. Just forget about it. You're better off eating something you found in the trash, really.

JAVERT HAS TROUBLE PARSING

JAVERT IS IN SLASH FICTION

JAVERT IS IN THE WRONG MUSICAL

SLOPPY LEADERSHIP

FIBER CRAZE

THE SWEATER ISSUE

WWII MOVIE

EITHER THE WALLPAPER GOES OR I DO

WWII MOVIE II

PEARSON

CALL ME MIKE

LESTER?! THAT'S NOT A NAME FOR AN AVIATION HERO, THAT'S A NERD NAME!

I'M CALLING YOU MIKE

CAN I KEEP THE BOWTIE

YOU'RE ALRIGHT MIKE

CANADA HATES ITS HEROES

WE'VE AVOIDED WAR IN THE SUEZ TODAY, THANKS IN NO SMALL PART TO THE EFFORTS OF MR. PEARSON AND HIS COLLEAGUES

I'M CERTAIN YOUR COUNTRY WILL GIVE YOU A HERO'S WELCOME

CANADA

CANADA NEWS

PEARSON DOES HE WANT A MEDAL OR SOMETHING?

NO ONE CARES, PG. 6

Pearson had the Little Minority Government That Could, giving people free health care, pensions, and student loans for the first time, among other achievements. He gave a lot to Canada, which we—correctly or not—like to claim as proof of some national character; he symbolizes the things we like about ourselves. If only we could go back in time now and tell that to the people who made fun of his lisp.

ELECTION

ALL THE WAY WITH LBJ

GET ME THE MOST EXPERIENCED ADVISORS IN THIS PARTY!

YES SIR

I DID NOT MEAN MACKENZIE KING'S DEAD TERRIERS

SHOO

WELL YOU ASKED

RED ENSIGN, ADIEU

PEARSON YOU SHUT YOUR LISPY MOUTH ABOUT THIS BLASPHEMOUS NEW FLAG ISSUE

BUT IT WILL BE UNIFYING - AND INDEPENDENT

LEAF FLAGS DON'T UNIFY CANADIANS

THEN WHAT DOES

THE BRITISH MONARCHY

I THINK THAT'S FOR UNIFYING BRITISH PEOPLE

BRAHMS'S FIRST IMPRESSION

How could Brahms have fallen asleep at a performance by Liszt? By most accounts the guy was all Jerry Lee Lewis on the piano, banging on the keys and kicking his legs and winking at the audience and making out with women all at the same time. You'd have to be already dead to fall asleep during that.

132

THE ADVENTURES OF SEXY BATMAN

MEET YOUR MATCH

GARTER

Batman is fun. Batman is *so much fun*, and that is why everyone makes comics about him, even though he's supposed to be scary and serious. Case closed. Everyone can make silly Batman comics now and feel good about it. Plus, did you really pick up this book for anything but Batman and butt drawings? A marriage of two fine things, like wine and more wine.

THE SLIP

FOILED AGAIN MISTA J
I KNOW
CURSE YOU SEXY BATMAN! YOU'RE TOO SLIPPERY
IT'S BECAUSE I AM COVERED IN VASELINE

BRUCE WAYNE

GOING OUT INCOGNITO TODAY ALFRED
VERY GOOD MASTER BRUCE
WELL I'M OFF

CARWASH

SHE'S MY CHERRY PIE
DO YOU COME WITH THE CAR
OH YOU

STAKE OUT

OFF TO DO SOME CRIMES
!
PENGUIN YOU'RE COMING WITH ME
I AM VERY UNCOMFORTABLE
Let's go

QUEEN BESS AT TILBURY

If you were at Tilbury and Queen Elizabeth, like, burst in there all up on a horse with some gnarly armor and she was yelling about how much she kicks ass and therefore you, as her subject, can do the same, maybe you too would feel like the Spanish Armada ain't no thang. In any case, it worked pretty well for her. On top of this, whenever someone tries to attack England by sea, they do it during Storm Week, which results in many wrecked ships and many more wrecked ambitions.

1980S BUSINESSWOMAN COMICS

I think these comics are mostly the product of my childhood understanding of business ladies. You see, I was born in the 1980s, when images of boxy-shouldered, helmet-haired, red-lipstick-wearing women were striding across magazines and TV shows in giant heels, and I guess they inserted themselves into the pantheon of jobs you one day figured you could have. You know, nurse, princess, teacher, businesswoman. From the images I was familiar with, I gathered that these women: (1) did business *all the time*, or (2) if they were not doing business, they were probably exercising. Pretty fierce, but also, it kind of rules.

OFFICE HOURS

DOUBLE TASK

REST

NANCYS

What mischief is Nancy Drew getting into? I've read all the books, so I can just tell you. Join me on a series of unforgettable adventures!

NANCY DREW MYSTERY STORIES
The Hidden Window Mystery
By CAROLYN KEENE
I NEED TO SOLVE A MYSTERY BUT THIS CAT IS IN THE WAY!
NANCY?
NANCY ARE YOU ALRIGHT?
GO AWAY CAT
NANCY
MISTER PRESIDENT!
OH NANCY..
Nancy Drew Mystery Stories
THE CLUE IN THE CRUMBLING WALL
By CAROLYN KEENE
OH MY GOD - THERE ARE MEN INSIDE THE WALL
WE'RE JUST ON THE OTHER SIDE
HOLD ON
NANCY'S COMING
WE COULD JUST WALK AROUND

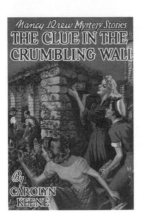

Nancy Drew Mystery Stories
THE SECRET OF RED GATE FARM
By CAROLYN KEENE

WHAT SECRET DANCE CLUB IS THIS?
I HAVE TO JOIN
NANCY DO YOU KNOW WHO THEY ARE
NO BUT I WILL
I AM CALLING YOUR P.R. DEPARTMENT

52 NANCY DREW MYSTERY STORIES
THE SECRET OF THE FORGOTTEN CITY
by CAROLYN KEENE

I'M SO EXCITED TO GO TO THE FORGOTTEN CITY! I'M GOING TO DO ALL THE SHOPPING
THIS MAP SAYS THE MALL IS ALSO FORGOTTEN
AW WHAT'S THE POINT

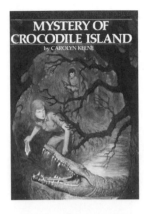

WHY, THIS ISLAND IS FULL OF CROCODILES!

THAT EXPLAINS SO **MUCH**

IT'S CALLED CROCODILE ISLAND

THIS WAS NOT A MYSTERY THAT NEEDED TO BE SOLVED

PUT ALL THE MONEY IN THE GROUND— I DON'T TRUST THE BANKS

I DON'T TRUST ANYONE

NANCY **NO**

HRK

BAM

THE GHOST OF BLACKWOOD HALL
by CAROLYN KEENE
I THINK THE GHOST IS TRYING TO TELL US SOMETHING THROUGH HIS MUSIC
BENNIE! BENNIE! BENNIE AND THE JEEETTSS
BUT WHAT COULD IT MEAN?

46 • NANCY DREW MYSTERY STORIES®
THE INVISIBLE INTRUDER
by CAROLYN KEENE
OH NED, I LOVE YOUR SKULL COLLECTION
OH NANCY, I KNEW YOU'D UNDERSTAND
THAT ONE IS JANICE, AND THAT ONE IS CLAIRE
GIRL NAMES
HA HA SHOULD I BE JEALOUS
YES

THE CROOKED BANISTER
by CAROLYN KEENE
NOW THAT I HAVE THIS CRIME SOLVING ROBOT, I CAN TAKE IT EASY
ROBOT, COMPUTE THE SOLUTION TO THE CROOKED BANISTER MYSTERY
BOOP BOOP BOOP
NOT NOW CRIME SOLVING ROBOT!
BOOP BOOP BOOP BOOP
NANCY WHY DON'T YOU LOVE ME
NANCY DREW MYSTERY STORIES
The Secret in the Old Attic
FINALLY!
THIS IS WHERE FATHER KEEPS THE MYSTERY JUICE

RASKOLNIKOV

Ah, the disenchanted young people of today, letting the things they read go to their heads. Folly of youth! It's everything your father warned you about when you said you were getting a philosophy degree. Why couldn't you just get a trade in plumbing? Everyone needs a plumber sooner or later! Now you've gone and embarrassed yourself by killing a few people for your new principles. What on earth are we going to tell the neighbours?

THROW THEM OFF THE TRAIL

BLUNT SIDE OF THE AXE BUT OH WELL

RAZUMIKHIN MY ONLY FRIEND

RASKOLNIKOV, YOU'RE SO ILL LOOKING! WHAT'S THE MATTER, LET ME HELP YOU WITH YOUR PROBLEM

NO!

BUT WE'RE FRIENDS!

HISSSS

THOUGH I COMPLETELY FORGET WHY

BUGGER OFF

ON CRIME

I FIRST SUSPECTED YOU, RASKOLNIKOV, WHEN I READ AN ARTICLE YOU WROTE

WHAT ARTICLE

MURDERING OLD LADIES: NOT EVEN A BIG DEAL
BY R. RASKOLNIKOV

YOU ARE CLEARLY LOOKING FOR SOMETHING THAT ISN'T THERE

SONYA, GET WITH THE PROGRAM

OH SONYA, IT'S ALL BEARING DOWN ON ME, I CAN'T TAKE IT

THE GUILT OF YOUR TERRIBLE CRIMES?

TERRIBLE?? SONYA, I DIDN'T DO ANYTHING WRONG, SOMETHING **ELSE** MUST BE BOTHERING ME

YOU'RE NOT A GREAT NAPOLEON MAN AND OBVIOUSLY YOU DON'T UNDERSTAND

SAY WHAT

siiighhh

SINCE YOU BROUGHT IT UP

SIR, SIR!! ARE YOU ALRIGHT, YOU LOOK CRAZY! DO YOU NEED WATER? IS THERE...

uuughhh

ARE THERE A COUPLE OF **MURDERS** YOU NEED TO CONFESS??

NO...

WELL ACTUALLY NOW THAT YOU MENTION IT

A BRAND NEW ERA

Do you think when the Middle Ages ended, they had town meetings and everyone was instructed, "Okay, set your watches—it's the dawn of a new era"? Of course not. That's silly. No one had watches in the Middle Ages. They'd have to adjust their sundials or adjust their general sense of guessing what time of day it is.

THE FAMOUS FITZGERALDS

So, I said I would work on something with the Fitzgeralds, and here they are in all their glory, ruining each other's dreams. First Zelda got a bad rap for mucking things up for Scott, then the other way around. But the truth is, they were both a big mess. Let's call it a tie.

GREAT GATSBYS

DREAM GIRL

Everyone has to read *The Great Gatsby* in high school because it's the best example of constructing a novel with themes and symbols, like legos, only not legos but The American Dream and the eyes of Dr. T.J. Eckleburg. Fifteen-year-olds can really get behind an essay on what the green light means, which is good, because they sure as heck won't relate to any of the characters, who are all huge jerks with enough money to be wasted most of the time on top of being miserable.

LIKE TOM'S A GOOD FATHER

IN THE VALLEY OF ASHES

GREEN LIGHT

MAN, GATSBY IS SO INTENSE WHEN HE STARES AT THAT LIGHT

I WONDER WHAT IT'S ALL ABOUT

...

I WISH THAT GREEN LIGHT DIDN'T GIVE ME SEIZURES

THE REAL JAY GATSBY

I HEARD GATSBY GOT HIS MONEY FROM THE GERMANS

I HEARD HE'S A RUSSIAN COUNT

WELL I HEARD HE'S SOME KIND OF HARSH CRITICAL METAPHOR

WHAT!

I DON'T THINK I **LIKE** THIS GUY

GOOD PARTY THOUGH

THAT'S PRETTY OLD

YOU CAN NEVER BE LIKE US, GATSBY. WE'RE OLD MONEY

WELL, HOW OLD?

SO OLD

OLD AS **BALLS**

LATER SHE DUMPS HIM

I'M JUST A NICE GUY, I DON'T REALLY JUDGE ANYBODY

THAT'S WHY I CAN DATE YOU, JORDAN, EVEN THOUGH YOU ARE AN ASSHOLE

AND I CAN BE FRIENDS WITH TOM EVEN THOUGH HE'S A RACIST, AND DAISY EVE...

YOU'RE TOO KIND

JUST AS GOOD THE SECOND TIME

NICK'S LUNCH DATE

HENRY'S LESSON

Wasn't it lucky for Henry that disagreeing with the Catholic Church and wanting to get rid of its power also meant pocketing a load of cash? Those monks were holy bros who prayed a lot, but they were also getting their Friar Tuck on in the Party Room of the Monasteries and Henry needed that wine money for wars and probably some wife-related funeral expenses.

HAMLET

IN MOURNING FOREVER

THE GHOST EXPLAINS

The play *Hamlet* is a case study in the behavior of depressed young dudes during the time before you could just let off steam by listening to Morrissey records in your bedroom with the lights turned off. How many monarchs has Morrissey really saved with his music? We may never know. But what is irrefutable is that there are many less regicides these days. A connection??

CLAUDIUS AND POLONIUS ARE THERE TOO

CLAUDIUS EXPOSES HIMSELF

LAERTES RETURNS

THE PRINCE OF NORWAY ARRIVES

SACAGAWEA AND YORK TRAVEL TO THE PACIFIC

NOW WE'LL NEVER GET THERE

BACK OF THE VAN

There are people who protest the fame of Lewis and Clark because their mission didn't really do what it was supposed to, and here we are plopping them into the pages of every grade-school textbook. The real benefit of reading about Lewis and Clark is the inclusion of people like Sacagawea and York in the narrative, who were not overly remarkable in a historical sense, but were ordinary people who stood out with their courage, skills, and conviction, and did not happen to be puffed-up, high-ranking white guys, of which we already have plenty.

PAPOOSE

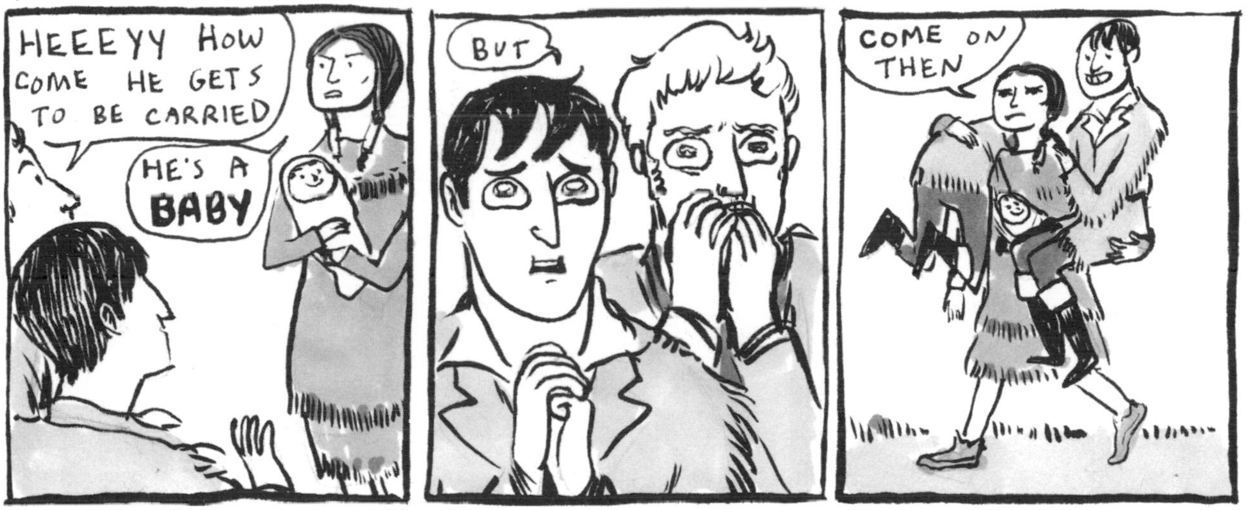
HEEEYY HOW COME HE GETS TO BE CARRIED
HE'S A BABY
BUT
COME ON THEN

EARN IT

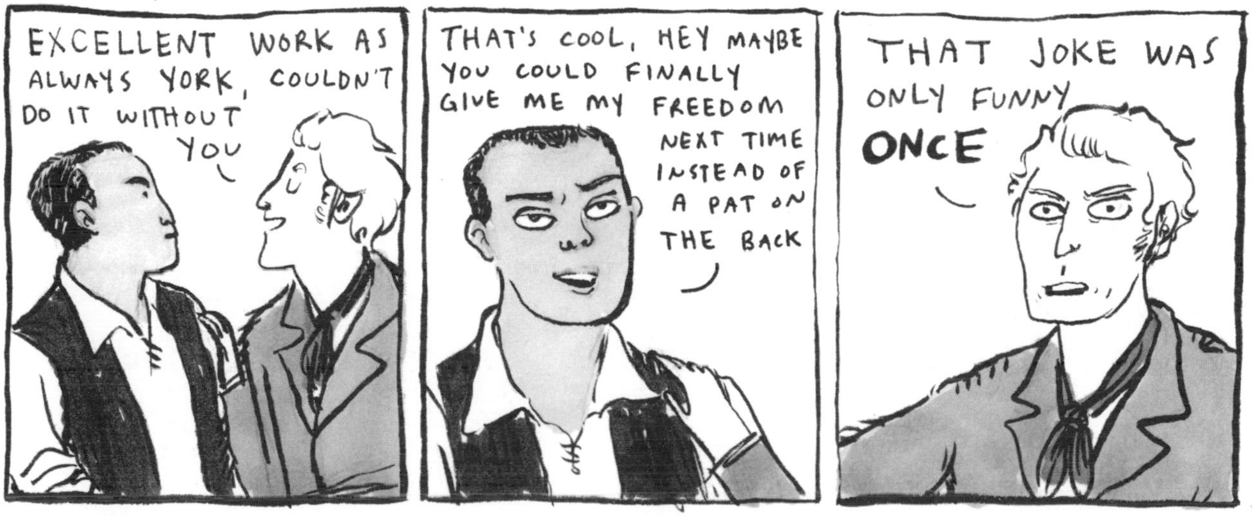
EXCELLENT WORK AS ALWAYS YORK, COULDN'T DO IT WITHOUT YOU
THAT'S COOL, HEY MAYBE YOU COULD FINALLY GIVE ME MY FREEDOM NEXT TIME INSTEAD OF A PAT ON THE BACK
THAT JOKE WAS ONLY FUNNY ONCE

CHARBONNEAU

DESTINATION

INDUSTRIAL REVOLUTION FUN

NEW LIVING CONDITIONS

WELL YOU'VE GOT TYPHUS, CHOLERA, CONSUMPTION AND A BIT OF THE POX ON TOP

YOU ALSO CAN'T AFFORD ME, I FORGET WHY I CAME HERE

SMUF

SILLY ME — ANYWAY GOOD LUCK DYING

THANK YOU DOCTOR

IN THE CLUB

SO, WHAT MAKES YOU THINK YOU'RE A GOOD FIT FOR THIS LUDDITE SOCIETY?

WELL, I SMASHES LOOMS, I SMASHES FRAMING, I SMASHES ANY KIND OF MACHINE REALLY

VERY GOOD

I BREAKS BUTTER CHURNS AND CLOCKS TOO IF YOU WANT TO GET THOROUGH

LET'S NOT GET **TOO** ZEALOUS

When Oliver Twist says to the man with the food pot, "Please sir, I want some more," we know he is speaking for all the poor little orphans, and our hearts melt. Just give the little nipper some gruel! Or gravel mixed with water, whatever it was they were being fed. When your parents say, "There are starving children in Africa" to make you eat your dinner, it can only go so far. I'd throw in, "One hundred and fifty years ago you'd be a chimney sweep and dead at twelve and no one would give a shit." More broccoli please!

PLUS, IT'S CHEAP

WORK IS GOOD FOR CHILDREN, IT BUILDS THEIR CHARACTER!

GETTING MANGLED IN MACHINERY IS GOOD FOR CHILDREN, IT BUILDS CHARACTER!

LOOK AT ALL THE CHARACTER THAT CHILD HAS, HE COULD BE PRIME MINISTER!

HE'S DEAD

PREVAILING ATTITUDES

THE REASON THAT THE POOR ARE IN A BAD STATE IS NOT BECAUSE SOCIETY IS FAILING THEM

HONESTLY

IS IT **MY FAULT** THAT THEY'RE DIRTY AND LAZY?

EXACTLY EXACTLY

HONESTLY, ONCE THE POOR JUST **STOP** BEING SO **GROSS** THEY'LL BE ABSOLUTELY FINE

SO TRUE

SITCOM, VICTORIAN STYLE

RATINGS SLUMP SOLUTION

TEEN DRAMA

If you read a Victorian joke book you may be surprised by what they found funny, which is nothing, unless it was racist or sexist, in which case: hilarious. Aw, just kidding, they also thought farts were funny. If they did have a joke it took them two hours to tell it though.

A VERY SPECIAL EPISODE

WACKY NEIGHBOURS

INDEX

Kate Beaton grew up in the Maritimes, specifically Cape Breton, Nova Scotia. She earned a bachelor's degree in history and anthropology at Mount Allison University. During her last two years in school, she contributed to the student newspaper, unexpectedly morphing her lifelong obsessions with literature, history, and drawing into very funny comics. In 2007, after prodding from friends, Beaton uploaded her first comics to her website, receiving acclaim that set her on the path to becoming one of the most successful and talked about new cartoonists of the past decade. She eventually self-published the now-sold-out book *Never Learn Anything From History*. Her comics have appeared in the *New Yorker*, *Harpers*, the *National Post*, and *The Best American Comics* anthology. She won the Doug Wright Award for Best Emerging Talent and has been nominated for the Harvey and Shuster awards. Her website is www.harkavagrant.com.